God Is One

The Bhagavad-Gita Explained with 114 Questions & Answers

By Kamlesh Patel

God Is One
The Bhagavad-Gita Explained with 114 Questions & Answers

Copyright © 2010 by Kamlesh Patel

All rights reserved. No part of this book may be reproduced or transmitted in any form or by any means without written permission from the author.

ISBN 9780982715017

Table of Contents

Contributors 4
Other works by the author 4
Dedication 4
Introduction 5
1. What is the Bhagavad-Gita? 6
2. What information does the Bhagavad-Gita give? 6
3. What does the Bhagavad-Gita teach? 6
4. What is the history of the Bhagavad-Gita? 7
5. What is the peace formula for the whole world? 7
6. What causes humans to hate each other? 8
7. When is self-defense necessary? 8
8. What is maya? 9
9. What are the qualities of God? 10
10. What is Yoga? 10
11. Does everything we have come from God? 11
12. Does God have a form? 11
13. Is there scientific basis for God having a form? 12
14. What is Religion? 12
15. What is the purpose of Religion? 13
16. Is the purpose of life to build an empire? 13
17. Do you worship idols? 14
18. Is God everywhere? 16
19. Who is Krishna? 16
20. Is Krishna a bully or a hater? 17
21. How brilliant does God look? 17
22. What is the kingdom of God like? 17
23. When is the Day of Judgment? 18
24. How does God witness all our actions? 18
25. Are we the body or the Soul? 18
26. Do we live forever? 19
27. What happens at death? 19
28. Are the dead waiting in their graves or gone? 20
29. Will I see my relatives again after this life? 20
30. Show me God, only then I will believe? 21
31. What body will you get next? 21
32. Is 2012 the end of the World? 22
33. Is freedom of religion the will of God? 22
34. How do I understand the reality of reincarnation? 23
35. What does rejecting karma and reincarnation mean? 24
36. How do we move up or down in Life? 25
37. How many species of living beings are there? 25
38. Are animals our brothers and sisters? 26
39. Is killing plants and animals the same? 26
40. Does Krishna bite? 26
41. What are the three gates to hell? 27
42. Who is the father of all living beings? 27

43. Who controls the heat and rain? 27
44. Is keeping pets bad for the pets and humans? 27
45. Is abortion bad or good? 28
46. Who is the origin of everything? 29
47. Who knows the past, present, and the future? 29
48. Why can't we remember our past lives? 29
49. Who is the greatest person? 30
50. How great is God? 30
51. What is Leather? 31
52. Can you digest your food? 31
53. Do you know the time? 31
54. Do you drink water in the light? 31
55. Why is life full of ups and downs? 32
56. Who are the Demigods? 32
57. How great are the Demigods? 32
58. Should the Demigods be worshipped? 33
59. Does Satan really exist? 33
60. What are the four Yugas (Ages)? 34
61. Is Bollywood demonic? 34
62. Is America the Supreme Destination? 35
63. Is a degree in medicine the king of Education? 36
64. What is the result of material education but no spiritual education?
.... 37
65. What is the caste system? 38
66. What is barbaric? 39
67. What takes away the good qualities in a person? 40
68. How do I achieve peace of mind? 40
69. How do I become happy? 41
70. Is life on all planets miserable? 41
71. What are the three modes of material nature? 42
72. Should we be kind and tolerant like a tree? 43
73. How can I go to the kingdom of God? 43
74. Is your mind your friend or your enemy? 43
75. What are the moral values of civilized humans? 44
76. Should we only eat fresh food? 45
77. Are wholesome foods good for us? 45
78. Are hot and salty foods bad for us? 45
79. Are same sex relationships wrong? 45
80. What is Bhakti Yoga? 46
81. What is human and animal consciousness? 47
82. Can you describe God? 48
83. What keeps people in ignorance? 50
84. What makes people engage in sinful activities? 50
85. What is foolishness? 50
86. What are the problems of material life? 51
87. What are the daily decisions we have to make? 52
88. What is karma? 53
89. Why do we suffer? 53

90. Why do good people suffer? 54
91. Why bad people don't suffer? 54
92. Are those who live in big houses very fortunate?..................... 54
93. How do we minimize the reactions to our actions?................... 55
94. What are the symptoms of a spiritual master? 55
95. Are women lower than men? 56
96. Why should women be protected from degradation?................ 57
97. What is the result of not following the scriptures? 57
98. How great are some Yogis? 57
99. Why should you be charitable? 57
100. What is the best charity?... 58
101. What is the highest service to God?.. 58
102. What is the difference devotees and yogis? 59
103. Why no intoxications? 59
104. Why no gambling?.. 60
105. Why no meat eating?.. 60
106. Why no Illicit sex? 60
107. What is the mentality of those who don't follow the Bhagavad-Gita?... 61
108. Does Krishna curse those who don't follow him?..................... 61
109. What is the mentality of those who follow the Bhagavad-Gita?. 62
110. What is a self-realized person?.. 62
111. What is the result of being Krishna conscious? 63
112. Who should I follow? 64
113. Will Krishna take away my sins?... 65
114. What is the difference between Krishna and others? 65

Contributors

Arjun K. Patel helped with graphic design.
Heran K. Patel helped with editing.

Other works by the author

Audio recordings of the Bhagavad-Gita As It Is on CDs in Sanskrit, English, Gujarati, Hindi, Spanish, French, and Arabic.

DVDs:

Bhagavad-Gita As It Is – English (over 14 hours on 4 DVDs).

Author Contact:

If you would like to distribute this book, please contact the author.
Email: info@gitamrta.org

Dedication

This book is dedicated to his divine grace A.C. Bhaktivedanta Swami Srila Prabhupada. Most of my knowledge realization comes from him and his followers.

Introduction

The aim of this book is to explain the teachings of an eternal scripture in a practical and easy to understand way.

The difference between this summarized Bhagavad-Gita and other versions is that this is practical, easier to understand, and without deviation from the original message of Lord Krishna.

We have questions and the Bhagavad-Gita has the answers, but to extract the answers to our questions from the Bhagavad-Gita, we would have to read it many times, and listen to many Swamis for many years. Then we might be able to get the answers to our questions. This book makes this easier and saves a lot of time, effort, and miseries. I give the questions that most people have in mind, and the answers based on the Bhagavad-Gita, using direct simple language.

I could not get the permission to use the translations by his divine grace A.C. Bhaktivedanta Swami Srila Prabhupada and so I did the Sanskrit to English translation myself. I have tried to explain the Sanskrit into English in a simple way, without deviating from the original message of Lord Krishna and Swami Srila Prabhupada's teachings.

The focus of this book is on the message of Lord Krishna to humanity and so I have omitted the statements in the translations, which address Arjuna, like 'O Arjuna', 'O son of Kunti', 'My dear Arjuna','O son of Bharata' and so on. This makes it clear that the message of the Bhagavad-Gita applies to everyone and not just to Arjuna.

Explanation of the Cover

The cover shows:

- God is one.
- God is a person with the most beautiful form.
- God is the most loving person.

1. What is the Bhagavad-Gita?

The Bhagavad-Gita is the conversation between a man called Arjuna, and God himself in the human form, Lord Krishna. It is the only scripture that can be called the word of God in person. This conversation last took place 5000 years ago in Kurukshetra, India.

The Bhagavad-Gita is questions from man (Arjuna) and answers from God (Lord Krishna).

2. What information does the Bhagavad-Gita give?

The Bhagavad-Gita gives information regarding God (Isvara), the living beings like you and me (the jivas), time (Kala), activities (karma), and material nature (Prakrti). No other scripture on the planet provides this information.

3. What does the Bhagavad-Gita teach?

Spiritual self-realization is the subject matter of the Bhagavad-Gita.

- There is only one God.
- The peace formula for the whole World.
- We are the soul, which is eternal. This means that just as we exist now, we existed before this life, and we will continue to exist after this body.
- How we can live eternally in the same body.
- God is the father of all living beings. This means all living beings are the children of God. We are all brothers and sisters. Thus we should not kill or hate any of our brothers and sisters (humans or animals). We have to love all living beings.
- We have to live a sinless life. This means; no meat eating, no gambling, no drinking, no smoking, no boyfriend/girlfriend, no cheating, no misleading others, no lying.
- How we can become peaceful and happy in this life.
- How brilliant God looks.
- How great God is.
- How Krishna is God.
- What are the qualities of civilized human beings.
- How does God witness all our actions.

- Bhakti Yoga.
- How we move up or down in species.
- How we can get through this miserable life.

4. What is the history of the Bhagavad-Gita?

Unlike the non-Vedic scriptures, the Bhagavad-Gita, is not a one off scripture, it's eternal. It was last spoken 5000 years ago by Krishna to Arjuna, and to the person who maintains the sun planet, Vivasvan, some 120 million years ago. It was first spoken in this universe in the current cosmic cycle, 155 trillion years ago.

Krishna appears once on this planet in every day of Brahma, which is every 8.64 billion years and each time, the Bhagavad-Gita is spoken by Krishna. So far in the current cosmic cycle alone, Krishna has appeared and spoken the Bhagavad-Gita over 17,939 times on this planet. The Bhagavad-Gita is also spoken in every universe, and there are millions of universes.

"I gave this science of self-realization knowledge to Vivasvan, and he gave it to Manu, and Manu gave the knowledge to his son, Iksvaku." (Lord Krishna, Bhagavad-Gita 4.1)

Vivasvan is a demigod who maintains the sun planet.

5. What is the peace formula for the whole world?

- All living beings including the animals are the children of the one God. This means we are all brothers and sisters.
- We are the soul and not the body. All souls are unique individuals, full of love, bliss, knowledge, and eternal.
- God is present in every living being. This means every living being is divine.

Anyone who seriously accepts these teachings, which are unique to the Bhagavad-Gita, would:

- Not hate or eat any of his brothers and sisters.
- Not kill or hurt any of his brothers and sisters.
- Love all his brothers and sisters.
- Become charitable and share his wealth with his unfortunate brothers and sisters.

"Those who are wise, have real knowledge, understanding, and gentleness. They see with equal vision, a Brahmana, a cow, an elephant, a dog, and a dog eater." (Lord Krishna, Bhagavad-Gita 5.18)

6. What causes humans to hate each other?

Due to bodily designations, we hate and fight each other.

We are the soul and not the body. The soul is not black or white. The soul is not Hindu, Christian, nor Muslim. The soul is not Indian or American or Iranian. The soul is not poor or diseased. The soul is not male or female. One soul is not inferior or superior to another.

All living beings are souls, part and parcel of God. We are all eternally, brothers and sisters. Every soul is a unique individual, full of bliss, knowledge, and eternal.

"All living entities are my eternal fragmental particles. Due to material nature, they are conditioned by the six senses, including the mind, and struggle very hard." (Lord Krishna, Bhagavad-Gita 15.7)

"One who does not hate anyone; is friendly and compassionate to all living beings; shares his belongings with others; has no sense of ownership; free from ego; even-minded in both happiness and distress; forgiving; tolerant in all situations; always satisfied; worships me with determination and devotion. Such a person is very dear to me." (Lord Krishna, Bhagavad-Gita 12.13-14)

7. When is self-defense necessary?

The Bhagavad-Gita was spoken on the battlefield and so one of its teachings is to know when self-defense is necessary. It was the will of Lord Krishna that all the soldiers on both sides, except for the Pandavas, would not go back home. It made no difference whether Arjuna took part in the war or not. Arjuna was merely an instrument that Lord Krishna used to destroy the soldiers on both sides. Even before the war started, Lord Krishna showed Arjuna, the soldiers being destroyed.

There have always been divine and demonic humans, since the beginning of creation in each cycle. Those who misuse the free will given by God are the demonic and those who properly use the free will are called the divine or demigods. The police and military in each country are not punished if they act according to the instructions of the government. In a similar way, God does not punish those who act to protect themselves from aggressors. There are five aggressors; those who give poison, those who set fire to a house, those who attack, those who steal land, and those who kidnap women. When one engages in violence to defend himself from these aggressors, there is no karmic reaction, as it is righteous to protect one's body, house, land, and women.

"All these warriors have already been put to death by my arrangement, you are merely an instrument that I am using. Just get up and fight, you will win over these aggressors." (Lord Krishna, Bhagavad-Gita 11.33)

The Bhagavad-Gita was spoken just before the start of Kali Yuga, the age of irreligion, ignorance, and aggressors. Until 5000 years ago, Vedic emperors from New Delhi ruled the whole World. Lord Krishna spoke the Bhagavad-Gita to instruct Arjuna and the followers of Vedic culture, but unfortunately the Temples and Swamis have failed to teach this important message of the Bhagavad-Gita. The result of this foolishness is that instead of Bharat ruling the whole World, the whole World is ruling Bharat. Bit by bit, the land of Bharat is being stolen by foreigners.

Vedic culture means no killing, no slavery, no hatred, universal brotherhood, no aggressors, no exploitation, and full knowledge of God.

Non-Vedic culture means killing, slavery, hatred, no universal brotherhood, aggressors, exploitation, and godlessness.

The simple fact is that the Hindus have not attacked other nations, never enslaved others, and never stolen land belonging to others. This is the result of following the culture created by God. The non-Hindus cannot say the same.

8. What is maya?

Maya has two meanings, compassion and illusion.

Maya is a state of mentality that makes us think that we can be happy by being materialistic and sinful. The aim of this illusionary energy is to keep us in the material creation, so we suffer. Maya is in the form of people with no spiritual knowledge, newspapers, TV, Internet, places, and so on. We should be very careful about all the things that are not spiritually related, by keeping away from them. Otherwise we will become materialistic and sinful, and stay in this miserable material creation for countless lifetimes.

9. What are the qualities of God?

God is the most powerful person, no one can defeat God in anyway.

God is the most beautiful person, no one is more beautiful than God.

God is the most famous person, he has been known for millions of years and on millions of planets.

God is the most merciful person, he doesn't send anyone eternally to hell.

God is the most forgiving person, he gives us unlimited chances and not just one (reincarnation).

God is the most caring person, he even cares for the animals like cows, pigs, chickens etc. (vegetarianism).

God is the fairest person, we are rewarded or punished based on our own actions (karma).

God is the most just person, he doesn't make one suffer or enjoy for no reason (karma).

God is the most efficient person, he doesn't keep the dead waiting (reincarnation).

God is the most responsible person, he doesn't order his followers to hate others.

God is the most renounced person, he is willing to fully share his creation with us.

Anyone who claims to be God, should have at least all the above qualities, otherwise he is not God. So far, only Krishna has proved that he has all the above qualities, not just once, but millions of times, as he has appeared millions of times.

10. What is Yoga?

Yoga means to link with the supreme person. There are many types of Yoga systems, but the top most Yoga system according to Lord Krishna in the Bhagavad-Gita is Bhakti Yoga, devotional service unto God.

The other types of yoga systems like Hatha Yoga involve bodily postures and breathing exercises. Hatha Yoga is for the body and Bhakti Yoga is for the soul. We need to maintain our body and soul and thus both are beneficial for us. But Bhakti Yoga is very important as our current body is only for this short life but the soul is eternal.

"Yoga is linking oneself with the Supreme. One can never become a yogi unless the desires for sense gratification are given up." (Lord Krishna, Bhagavad-Gita 6.2)

11. Does everything we have come from God?

Yes, we have the same qualities that God has, but in a minute quantity.

We have a form, because God has a form.
We are beautiful to some degree, because God is most beautiful.
We are powerful to some degree, because God is most powerful.
We have some knowledge, because God has all knowledge.
We have some intelligence, because God has all intelligence.
We are merciful to some degree, because God is most merciful.
We love to some degree, because God is all loving.
We are peaceful to some degree, because God is most peaceful.
We are caring to some degree, because God is most caring.
We can remember some things from our childhood, because God can remember everything from everyone's past.

12. Does God have a form?

Yes, God has a form. You have a form, the plants and animals have a form, so why shouldn't the person from whom all forms originate have a form?

Your father has a form, your grandfather had a form, and your great grandfather had a form. In this way, if you go back to the original person, from whom we all originate, God, he also has a form, and that's why we have a form.

"Foolish men, disregard me when I appear in a human like body. They do not know that my nature is spiritual, and I am the great Lord of everything. (Lord Krishna, Bhagavad-Gita 9.11)

"Although I am unborn, imperishable, eternal, and the Lord of all living beings, using my internal energy, I still appear in my original spiritual form [human like form]." (Lord Krishna, Bhagavad-Gita 4.6)

Krishna appears in his original form once in every day of Brahma, which is every 8.64 billion years. So far in the current cycle, Krishna has appeared more than 17,939 times on this planet in his original spiritual form.

13. Is there scientific basis for God having a form?

If God can deliver his message, then from a scientific analysis, there must be some intelligent noise, which must be produced by some intelligent vibrations, which must come from the mouth of an intelligent living being. If there is a mouth, then there must be ears, nose, chest, hands, and legs. Thus God must be a person with a form, if he can deliver his message.

If one thinks that God does not have a form, then it means there are no legs, no hands, no chest, no nose, no ears, no mouth, no vibrations, and no message. This means there is no God (atheistic).

Can you love an invisible person? The simple answer is no.
Can you serve an invisible person? The simple answer is no.
Can you show your love to someone you have not seen, for example someone in the womb? The simple answer is no.

14. What is Religion?

To follow the teachings or laws of God is called religion. Since God is eternal, the religion or teachings of God must also be eternal.

- God is eternal, meaning he has always existed.
- If God has eternally existed then Man must also have eternally existed. Why would God live alone?
- The laws created by God for man to follow (religion) must have also eternally existed.
- The teachings of God are the scriptures, which must have also eternally existed.

That eternal religion which was created by the eternal God is called Sanatan Dharma, which literally means the 'eternal religion', which is also known as the Vedic religion or pure Hinduism. The eternal teachings of God are known as the Vedic scriptures.

If you read all the documents on the planet, you will find that the person, who has eternally been known by man to be God, is Lord Krishna.

The Vedic religion has been proven to be the oldest on the planet, and the oldest scriptures on the planet are the Vedic scriptures, which were written in the oldest language known to man, Sanskrit, the most systematic language on the planet, the best language.

Why follow recently created man made scriptures, when you can follow eternal scriptures like the Bhagavad-Gita. Why follow an unknown, unproven, or invisible God, when you can follow a known, proven, and visible God, Lord Krishna.

Lord Krishna gave the Vedic knowledge to Brahma, the first living being created in each universe, at the beginning of each cycle. In the current cycle, this was 155.522 trillion years ago. Lord Krishna gave the Vedic knowledge again, just 5000 years ago, to Arjuna.

"I am telling you this ancient science of linking with the Supreme [Yoga], because you are my friend and devotee. Therefore you can understand the mystery of this highest science." (Lord Krishna, Bhagavad-Gita 4.3)

15. What is the purpose of Religion?

The purpose of religion is to know, serve, and love God. But you can only serve and love someone, if you know him or her. You cannot serve or love an invisible or unknown person. Only the Vedic scriptures describe exactly who the person God is. The non-Vedic scriptures don't have a clue as to who God is. Serving and loving God includes serving and loving all God's creatures. This means serving and loving all humans and animals. We should not hurt or eat any of our brothers and sisters, the animals are also our brothers and sisters.

Can anyone love an invisible person? No.

16. Is the purpose of life to build an empire?

Life after life we are working like donkeys to build our empire of properties, big bank balances, nice cars, college degrees, and so on. But at the end of each life, we have to give everything up. We can't transfer our bank balance from one life to another, nor can be take our material educational qualifications like a degree in medicine with us to our next life. Nor can we take our properties or family members with us. In each life we have to start all over again.

While we are busy working hard to build our empire, we forget that there is time, which is taking away our life. A sword is hanging over your head and at any moment it will drop, then you (the soul) will be transferred to another body and you will then have to start all over again from scratch.

Those who are intelligent will work hard to make a living but they will also gain some spiritual knowledge so eventually they gain enough to go back to the spiritual abode where we live in the same beautiful body. That is eternal, full of bliss, and full of knowledge.

17. Do you worship idols?

No. We don't worship idols but deities of God. God is a person with a form, and he wants to be worshipped in an image form. This can be proven by the fact that it's God who has been creating those who worship him in the image form for millions of years, the Hindus. And the same God has been creating those who don't worship him in the image form, the non-Hindus, for only a few thousand years at most.

Thus it's God's will that those who worship him in the image form are eternal (the Hindus) and those who cannot understand God having a form or those who are against image worship are not eternal.

If you read all the scriptures on the planet, you will learn that except for the Hindus, no other race or religious group has existed for more than a few thousand years. The Hindus have existed for millions of years and all other races originate from the Hindus. This is the will of God.

* The Muslims bow down to the black stone in the Kaaba when they pray.
* The Christians face the cross when they pray.
* The learned Hindus, face a deity of Lord Krishna when they pray.

Which is better? To face a black stone, a cross, or a real person while praying? Who are the idol worshippers?

Those who follow recently created, man-made religions cannot understand or know God as a person. This can be proven by the fact that some believe that God is invisible. This basically means they cannot know God. Some accept that God has a form, but they have no idea who he is. This also means they do not, and cannot know God.

It's not just the non-Hindus who are forbidden to worship God in an image form. The Hindus who eat meat are also forbidden to worship God in an image form as the animal killers, are considered too sinful to worship or know God directly as a person. For this same reason, other animal killers (non-Hindus) are not allowed to worship or know God as a person with a form. For the killers, God will always remain invisible and unknown.

"I am not manifest to everyone. The foolish persons are covered by my internal potency [Yoga Maya] and they cannot understand that I am unborn, and eternal, with a spiritual form." (Lord Krishna, Bhagavad-Gita 7.25)

The deities will appear as stone or wood to those who are not qualified to know God. But for the sincere devotees of God, the deities are real, and on many occasions, the deities actually come alive. But God is not cheap, he cannot be known by everyone, especially the yavanas and mlechhas (animal killers).

"All living beings are in utter ignorance from birth. They are deluded, due to hate and desires. Those persons whose sinful activities have come to an end, and are now pious, free from hate and desires, are able to engage in devotional service unto me with determination." (Lord Krishna, Bhagavad-Gita 7.27-28)

As stated in this verse, we are all born into delusion and are bewildered. But those who stop all sinful activities like animal killing, gambling, lust, alcohol, tobacco, drugs, and hatred, are freed from delusion, and only they can know God as a person and engage in his service.

Krishna is not a bully or hater of anyone. Krishna is nice. He loves all living beings.

"Even if you are the greatest sinner, when you are on the boat of spiritual knowledge, you will be able to cross over the river of miseries, caused by reactions to sinful activities." (Lord Krishna, Bhagavad-Gita 4.36)

Animal killers are considered very sinful, but Krishna is so merciful, even the most sinful person can go back to the spiritual creation (Vaikuntha) where they can live eternally in the same beautiful body, full of bliss, full of knowledge, with no problems, and no killing (no meat eating).

The fact is that worship of deity is worship of God. This can be proven by the fact that deity worshippers are peaceful, and non-violent. This is the result of pleasing God. Have you heard of a terrorist who is a deity worshipper? How many times have you heard of terrorists, who are not deity worshipper?

"Being freed from attachments, fear, anger, and fully situated in thought of me, many have become purified by penance and knowledge of me. They all attained pure love for me. (Lord Krishna, Bhagavad-Gita 4.10)

The purpose of religion is to achieve love of God. In this verse, Krishna states that those who worship him are freed from material attachments, fear, anger, become purified, and achieve pure love of God.

18. Is God everywhere?

Yes, Krishna is omnipresent, meaning he is present everywhere.

Those who are against deity worship limit the greatness of God. As they cannot understand that God is all pervading. This means God must be present everywhere, including within the deities.

Although Lord Krishna is always present on his supreme spiritual planet called Goloka Vrndavana, he is also present in the heart of every living being as the super soul, and he is present in every atom. This is how great Krishna is. But one should not think that everything is God.

If God is present everywhere then he has to be present in the atom, otherwise we cannot say God is present everywhere.

"The Supreme person is greater than all, and although he is present on his supreme abode, he is also present everywhere, and is attainable by unalloyed devotion." (Lord Krishna, Bhagavad-Gita 8.22)

19. Who is Krishna?

Krishna is God. Krishna has appeared millions of times in the past and each time he appears, many demonic living beings challenge him and Krishna very easily defeats them all. Also, every time he appears, Krishna saves all his followers. This is simple proof that he is the one and only God.

"I am the origin of all creations. There is nothing, moving or non-moving, that can exist without me." (Lord Krishna, Bhagavad-Gita 10.39)

There are many who claim to be God, or their followers claim them to be God. But how many of them, can actually say how they are God. Krishna very clearly states how he is God, and he also proved it. Full details can be found in the Srimad Bhagavatam.

20. Is Krishna a bully or a hater?

Krishna is not a mean God. He does not bully or hate anyone, nor does he order his followers to hate others. Krishna is nice. He is equal to all living beings, who are his children, and he loves all his children. Krishna advises his followers to be friendly to all living beings.

"I hate no one. I am equal to all living beings..." (Lord Krishna, Bhagavad-Gita 9.29)

"...One who has no enemies among all living beings comes to me." (Lord Krishna, Bhagavad-Gita 11.55)

"One who is compassionate to all living beings ... - These are some of the qualities of those born with divine nature." (Lord Krishna, Bhagavad-Gita 16.1-3)

21. How brilliant does God look?

"If many thousands of suns were to rise all at once in the sky, the radiance produced by this, might resemble the effulgence of the great Lord." (Arjuna, Bhagavad-Gita 11.12)

This is one of the greatness of Krishna that no one else can exhibit.

22. What is the kingdom of God like?

There are millions of planets with living beings in the material world, which represents 25% of the total creation. The other 75% is the spiritual creation, called Vaikuntha. On the millions of Vaikuntha planets, the people have the same features as Lord Narayan, who is an expansion of Lord Krishna. They are very beautiful, full of bliss, full of knowledge, four handed, and live an eternal life without a trace of anxiety. This means no financial problems, no taxes, no terrorism, no natural disasters, no marital problems, no disease, no old age, and no death.

"My supreme abode is not illuminated by the sun, moon, fire, or electricity. Those who go there, never come back to this material creation." (Lord Krishna, Bhagavad-Gita 15.6)

23. When is the Day of Judgment?

The Day of Judgment is immediately at death.

Why should God keep the dead waiting?
Some people have been dead for millions of years, why should God keep them waiting for so long?

God is very efficient he doesn't keep the dead waiting. At death, we are instantly judged according to the actions we have taken in life.

24. How does God witness all our actions?

God is with us 24 hours a day, 7 days a week. He is the witness to all your actions, and on the Day of Judgment, which is immediately at death; the perfect Judge (God) will sentence you without making any mistakes.

"I am the witness..." (Lord Krishna, Bhagavad-Gita 9.18)

"In the body, there is also the super soul. He is the master, supreme enjoyer, overseer, and the permitter - The supreme Lord." (Lord Krishna, Bhagavad-Gita 13.23)

Krishna is the super soul, seated in the heart of every living being.

25. Are we the body or the Soul?

We are the soul. The soul is present in the heart of every living being. Although so minute, the soul is so powerful that it animates the entire body with consciousness. It is situated in the heart, and when it leaves the body, the heart stops beating, as a result the blood stops circulating and the entire body disintegrates. There are 8.4 million different species of living beings that each individual soul can reside in.

"Just as the sun illuminates the whole universe with light, the soul illuminates the whole body with consciousness." (Lord Krishna, Bhagavad-Gita 13.34)

"The soul is unborn, eternal, never takes birth, and never dies. The soul is not destroyed when the body is destroyed." (Lord Krishna, Bhagavad-Gita 2.20)

The body is temporary, but we (the soul) are eternal. The body can be destroyed but nobody can destroy the soul.

26. Do we live forever?

Yes. We are eternal.

"There was never a time when you, all these kings, and I did not exist. Nor shall any of us cease to exist in the future. The embodied soul in this body goes through boyhood, youth, and old age. At death, the soul transfers to another body. This never bewilders a wise person." (Lord Krishna, Bhagavad-Gita 2.12-13)

Just as you exist now, you existed in the past, and you will continue to exist in the future.

There is a simple law of physics, which states that energy cannot be destroyed but it changes forms. We (the soul) are the energy and the body is the form. When our body is finished, we will change our form. Thus we get a new body. This is one of the simple proofs of reincarnation.

27. What happens at death?

At death, you (the soul) are immediately judged and then transferred to the womb of a particular mother in a particular universe, on a particular planet, in a particular country, in a particular city, on a particular street, in a particular home, exactly according to what you deserve.

"Just as a person gives up old and worn out garments for new garments. In a similar way, the embodied soul accepts new bodies, giving up the old and useless ones." (Lord Krishna, Bhagavad-Gita 2.22)

We change clothes, furniture, countries, jobs, wives/husbands, houses, friends, cars and so on. In a similar way, we will change bodies.

If you lived a pious life and gained spiritual knowledge, then you will not take birth again in the material creation. You will go to the spiritual creation called Vaikuntha, where you will eternally live in the same beautiful body, with no old age, no disease, no death, and no anxiety.

"Those who without deviation, meditate upon me, worship me, fix their mind on me, and become attached to me, I very quickly deliver them from material existence, which is an ocean of birth, death, and miseries." (Lord Krishna, Bhagavad-Gita 12.6-7)

28. Are the dead waiting in their graves or gone?

All the dead are neither waiting in their graves nor gone. God is very efficient, he doesn't keep anyone waiting nor does he waste anyone. All the dead are alive right now.

"The fact is that one who has taken birth, will certainly die. It is also a fact that, one who dies will take birth again. Therefore, you should not lament for that which is unavoidable." (Lord Krishna, Bhagavad-Gita 2.27)

Anyone can see that every second, living beings are dying and every second, living beings are being born. This is the transmigration of the soul from one body to another. This is another simple proof of reincarnation.

29. Will I see my relatives again after this life?

Never.

Our relationships are based on the body and so when the body is finished, our relationship is also finished forever. The body is destroyed after death and so we can never know that person again. Even if we come across the same soul again in another body, we will not know that this person was once in another body that we knew.

Arjuna was lamenting for his relatives who were on the opposing side of the war, and Krishna made him realize that all those relatives were never your relatives before this life and they will never be your relatives again, after this life.

We cannot know where the souls of our dead relatives and friends have gone. But there are some yogis and personalities like Brahma and Shiva, who can tell where the souls have taken birth again, and Krishna knows exactly where you and I were trillions of years ago.

In the material creation, all your friends and relatives are just for this life. But in the spiritual creation (Vaikuntha), you will know all your friends and relatives forever.

"The soul which resides in the body never dies. Therefore you should not lament for any living being." (Lord Krishna, Bhagavad-Gita 2.30)

30. Show me God, only then I will believe?

Is God your servant? If you want to see God, then you have to accept his terms and not yours.

"By performing devotional service unto me [Krishna], without deviation. You can begin to understand my mysteries, and thus I can be seen in this form, standing before you." (Lord Krishna, Bhagavad-Gita 11.54)

Most of us can't even meet the President of a small country on this insignificant planet. So how can we meet the President of millions of universes?

31. What body will you get next?

Your consciousness at death will determine your next body. This life is a preparation for the next. During each day of this life, you are developing a particular type of consciousness, which will manifest into a particular body at death. It's just like a manufacturing company designing its products today to produce tomorrow.

It's very easy to determine what your next body will be:

* If you have eaten animals, then you will become an animal and be eaten.
* If you are full of hate and anger towards others, then you will become an aggressive animal.
* If you have cursed others with a life of hell. Then you will end up in hell.
* If you like to expose your body, then you will become a tree, naked and exposed to all.
* If you like to eat everything and anything, then you will become a hog, who eats anything and everything.
* If you are attached to a dog, then you will become one (a dog).
* If you are friendly to all living beings, then you will get another human body.
* If you are friendly to all living beings and know who God is and serve him. Then you will be finished with material life and go back

to the kingdom of God (Vaikuntha). Where you will eternally live and play with God.

"Just as the air carries a particular smell from one place to another, the living entity will be carried to a particular body at death, based on the consciousness developed by him during life. On taking a new body, the living entity will get a particular set of senses, like ears, eyes, tongue, smelling potency, sense of touch, and mentality. The foolish persons cannot understand how a living entity quits one body to take another. But those with knowledge can see this." (Lord Krishna, Bhagavad-Gita 15.8-10)

32. Is 2012 the end of the World?

No.

There are cycles of creation and annihilation. The duration of each cycle is 311 trillion, 40 billion years. In the current cycle, the universe has existed for 155.522 trillion years old and it will end after 155.518 trillion years.

"At the end of each cycle [of 311 trillion years], all living beings enter into my material nature. At the beginning of a new cycle, I create them again by my potency." (Lord Krishna, Bhagavad-Gita 9.7)

This universe will be here for another 155.518 trillion years. But you won't be, your life may end at any time. So make sure you live a sinless life, so you move up in life (species) and not down.

33. Is freedom of religion the will of God?

Yes. God is in full control and by his will the people of various religions are being created every second.

Thus by not allowing freedom of religion, one is acting against the will of God. Those who are against the will of God, are called the faithless or envious of God.

"Those who are envious, cruel, full of hate, and wicked, are the lowest among men. I repeatedly cast these evildoers into the wombs of demonic species. Such persons are foolish and can never approach me. Birth after birth, they enter into the wombs of demonic species, and gradually sink down to the lowest state of life." (Lord Krishna, Bhagavad-Gita 16.19-20)

34. How do I understand the reality of reincarnation?

* When someone dies, we say 'He has passed away'. This implies that we accept that the soul and the body are different. The dead body is present before us but the soul has passed on. Where to? Another body.

* Every second living beings are dying and every second living beings are born. The souls in the dead bodies are being transferred to the new bodies. This is proof of the transmigration of the soul from one body to another.

* In scientific terms, energy cannot be destroyed, but it changes forms. Our body is the form and we (the soul) are the energy. When this current form of ours (this body) is destroyed. We (the soul) will change our form. Thus get a new body.

* Take a look around. Why are there varieties of conscious living beings? Why is one soul in the body of an animal and another soul in a human body? Why is one soul in the body of a female and another in a male body? Why is one soul born in China and another born in Africa and so on? The soul is moving from one body to another, life after life. The variation of bodies is simple proof of the transmigration of the soul from one body to another.

* The fact that God is merciful is proof of reincarnation. If God is merciful then why would he create some who are fortunate and some who are unfortunate in their one and only life? If after this one and only life we eternally go to hell or heaven, which is what the non-Vedic religions preach. Then how can God be merciful to those who are eternally sent to hell for messing up their one and only life. The fact that God is merciful is proof that he gives us unlimited chances and not just one. Thus we (the soul) transmigrate from one body to another life after life.

* If this is the only life, then why do we exist today and some will exist in the future and some existed in the past. The fact is that we exist today, we existed in the past, and we will exist in the future too.

* The body is temporary but the soul is eternal. Accept this fact? Yes? When this body is finished the soul must continue to exist, as it's eternal. And just as the soul is currently residing in this body,

when this body is finished the soul will continue to exist by residing in another body.

* If a sinner is sent to hell forever after only one life, then how can God be forgiving unless he is given another chance? The fact is that we get unlimited chances and not just one. This is because God is all-merciful.

35. What does rejecting karma and reincarnation mean?

If there is no reincarnation, then it means this is the one and only life.

Some people are born with cancer, in their only life.
Some people are born poor, in their only life.
Some people only live for a day and die, in their only life.
Some people suffer more than others, in their only life.
Some people are born blind, in their only life.

The above means God is very mean and not fair to those who are unfortunate. Or everything happens by chance, which means God is not in control. Both of these statements imply there is no God (atheistic).

Some people believe that they can live a life of sin, then at death they will be buried, and on some unknown day of judgment they will rise from their grave in the same body they died. They will get a bailout plan for their sins and then go to heaven and eternally live in the same body they died in. They can't get a new body, as this would mean reincarnation.

The above means that in heaven, there will be many old people as they died in their old age. Is living in an old body eternally, heavenly or hellish life?

Why should God keep the dead waiting (for the Day of Judgment), in some cases for millions of years? This means God is not very efficient.

Some people believe that only the followers of their religion go to heaven, the others eternally go to hell. This means God is not merciful or forgiving.

The believers of God must accept that God is merciful, fair, forgiving, and efficient. Thus those who reject karma and reincarnation are the unbelievers of God (atheists).

36. How do we move up or down in Life?

By getting a good education, earning good money, having a big house, and nice cars, you have simply become a polished animal. Material advancement is not evolution, but devolution of consciousness.

At death, all our degrees, properties, cars, and bank balances are completely useless. If you have spiritual knowledge, then you will move up in life, thus take birth in one of the higher species of living beings or overcome the cycle of birth and death. If you have no spiritual knowledge, then you will go down in life by taking birth in the lower species, in the plant and animal kingdoms.

There are 8.4 million species of living beings. According to exactly what you deserve, you will either go up or down in species after this life. I am not saying that you give up all the comforts of life and live in a cave, no. My point is that if you add some spirituality to your life, which includes stopping sinful activities like meat eating, gambling, drinking, and boyfriend/girlfriend business. Become charitable and treat people nicely. Then at least, you will be able to maintain your current position in your next life.

"At death, those who have developed the mode of goodness, will go to the higher planets where the saintly persons live. Those who have developed the mode of passion, will take birth among those engaged in materialistic activities. Those who have developed the mode of ignorance, will take birth in the animal kingdom." (Lord Krishna, Bhagavad-Gita 14.14-15)

"Those who are situated in the mode of goodness, go to the heavenly planets. Those in the mode of passion will take birth on planets like Earth. Those in the mode of ignorance will take birth on the hellish planets or in the animal kingdom." (Lord Krishna, Bhagavad-Gita 14.18)

37. How many species of living beings are there?

There are 8.4 million different species or bodies that the soul can reside in. Not all the species are present on this planet.

900,000 species of aquatic
2,000,000 species of plants
1,100,000 species of insects
1,000,000 species of birds
3,000,000 species of beasts
400,000 species of human beings

38. Are animals our brothers and sisters?

Yes. All living beings including the animals and plants have a soul, and are created by the one God. Consciousness is a sign of the existence of the soul, and thus the animal and plant bodies also have souls. They are our brothers and sisters, that's why we should not eat our helpless brothers and sisters, the animals. The heart of every living being contains the individual soul, and the super soul, Krishna.

"I am the super soul, situated within the heart of all living beings. I am the origin, the middle, and the end of all living beings." (Lord Krishna, Bhagavad-Gita 10.20)

We should not destroy the plant life in our gardens. Instead plant more fruit, vegetable, and flower bearing plants in our gardens.

39. Is killing plants and animals the same?

Cutting the throat of chickens and cutting grass isn't the same. When we take the fruits and vegetables, in most cases we don't actually kill the plant. We are just taking a by-product of the plants. For example, when we take an apple off a tree, we are not killing the apple tree. But when we take the leg of a chicken, we are killing the chicken.

40. Does Krishna bite?

Anyone can approach Krishna, as he doesn't bite. Krishna is a pure vegetarian he doesn't eat the flesh of animals. His followers must also not eat meat, fish, eggs, or buy leather.

"If a pure hearted person, offers me with devotion, a leaf, flower, fruit, or water. I will accept it." (Lord Krishna, Bhagavad-Gita 9.26)

We should offer all plant foods to God before we eat. So in this way, we will be released from any sins we unknowingly commit while obtaining food from plants.

"The righteous persons eat food that is first offered to me. They are released from all kinds of sins. But those who don't offer food to me before eating, are committing sin." (Lord Krishna, Bhagavad-Gita 3.13)

41. What are the three gates to hell?

"Lust, anger, and greed are the three gates that leads one to hell. One must give up these qualities." (Lord Krishna, Bhagavad-Gita 16.21)

The motivation for most crimes can be linked to lust, anger, and/or greed.

42. Who is the father of all living beings?

Krishna is the father of all living beings.

"All species of living beings in this material creation appear by taking birth, and I am the seed giving father." (Lord Krishna, Bhagavad-Gita 14.4)

"I am the father of the universe, the supporter, the mother, and the grandfather. I am the purifier, the sacred syllable 'aum', and the object of knowledge. I am also the Rig, Sama, and Yajur Vedas." (Lord Krishna, Bhagavad-Gita 9.17)

43. Who controls the heat and rain?

Krishna is the supreme controller.

"I control the heat. I withhold and send forth the rain. I am immortality, and death. I am spirit and matter." (Lord Krishna, Bhagavad-Gita 9.19)

44. Is keeping pets bad for the pets and humans?

Would you like to live in a cage?
Would you like to live in an air pocket in the water?
Would you like to be locked up all your life?
Would you like to be deprived of socializing with others?

No?

Well, do you think the helpless birds love to live in a small cage all their life?

Do you think fish love being locked up in a small air pocket (tank) all their life?

Do you think dogs love to be deprived of socializing with their own kind and living their natural life?

If you love animals like dogs, cats, birds, fish, and others. Then let them be free by allowing them to live in their own natural environment.

Some people think that by keeping their pet in their 5 star home is better than the jungle for the pet. Well, would you choose to live in a 7 star hotel alone, or with your family in a hut?

Another reason why you should not keep pets is that, if at the time of death, you think of them, then you will become one. This means that if you think of your dog at the time of death, then you will get a dog's body, without fail. Then the humans will pick up your stool, if you live in America.

"Whatever nature, one has at the time of death. That nature he will attain without a doubt." (Lord Krishna, Bhagavad-Gita 8.6)

If you have served a dog in your life then you will naturally think of a dog at the time of death. Thus you will attain a dog's nature, which is 4 legs and barking. If you have served God in your life then you will naturally think of God at the time of death. Thus you will attain Krishna's nature, which is a beautiful body, full of bliss, full of knowledge, and eternal.

"Whoever thinks of me [Krishna] at the end of life, attains my nature, without a doubt." (Lord Krishna, Bhagavad-Gita 8.5)

45. Is abortion bad or good?

Very bad.

Would a mother kill a child she has seen? No! Just because the child is in the womb and not seen, does it mean that the child is not the mothers' or does it mean the child is not alive in the womb?

From the second a woman becomes pregnant, a new soul has entered into the woman's womb. This means a unique living being with consciousness is now in the womb of the mother.

Only a stonehearted mother would kill this unique living being without seeing it and giving it a chance of life.

"All living entities are my eternal fragmental particles. Due to material nature, they are conditioned by the six senses, including the mind, and struggle very hard." (Lord Krishna, Bhagavad-Gita 15.7)

All living beings belong to God, and thus we have no right to take away life.

46. Who is the origin of everything?

Krishna is the origin of everything.

"I am the origin of all creations. There is nothing, moving or non-moving, that can exist without me." (Lord Krishna, Bhagavad-Gita 10.39)

"I am the origin of the whole creation. Everything emanates from me. The wise worship me [Krishna] with devotion." (Lord Krishna, Bhagavad-Gita 10.8)

"All living beings have their source from my material and spiritual energies, and know for certain that I am the origin and dissolution of the entire creation." (Lord Krishna, Bhagavad-Gita 7.6)

47. Who knows the past, present, and the future?

Krishna is omniscient. Meaning he knows the past, present, and the future.

"I completely know the past, the present, and the future. I also know all living beings, but no one really knows me." (Lord Krishna, Bhagavad-Gita 7.26)

48. Why can't we remember our past lives?

It's for our own good that we don't know our past lives. We have so many problems in this life, knowing our past will only add more worries, and make our current life more miserable.

"Arjuna, you and I have taken many births. I can remember all of them, but you cannot." (Lord Krishna, Bhagavad-Gita 4.5)

49. Who is the greatest person?

Krishna is omnipotent, meaning he is the greatest.

"There is nothing superior to me. Everything is resting upon me. Just like pearls are strung on a thread." (Lord Krishna, Bhagavad-Gita 7.7)

"I am transcendental, beyond the fallible and infallible, and because I am the best, I am celebrated as the Supreme person, on the material, and spiritual planets, and in the Vedas." (Lord Krishna, Bhagavad-Gita 15.18)

50. How great is God?

It would take over 400 billion nuclear weapons to produce the same amount of heat that the sun produces in just 1 second, and the sun has been giving this heat for millions of years, and there are millions of suns, one in each universe.

"The light of the sun, which illuminates the entire universe, and the light of the moon and fire, all come from me." (Lord Krishna, Bhagavad-Gita 15.12)

"With a single particle of myself [Krishna], I maintain the entire creation." (Lord Krishna, Bhagavad-Gita 10.42)

Many people say God is great but they have no idea how great he is. In the above verses, Krishna is stating that he is the maintainer and controller of the sun, moon, and the entire creation. Krishna in his Maha Vishnu expansion has millions of universes coming out of his body with every exhalation, and with every inhalation, millions of universes go back into his body.

"Everything that is opulent, beautiful, and glorious, is created from a spark of my splendor." (Lord Krishna, Bhagavad-Gita 10.41)

All that is great comes from a single spark of Krishna.

51. What is Leather?

Leather items like sofas, car seats, jackets, handbags, and chair covers, are mainly made from cows. This means cows are killed so you can sit on them or wear them. Don't buy leather; buy cloth sofas, cloth car seats, cloth clothing, and cloth bags.

52. Can you digest your food?

If you can digest your food then you accept Krishna, as Krishna is the fire of digestion.

"I am in the bodies of all living beings as the fire of digestion. I unite with the ingoing and outgoing air, and I digest the food." (Lord Krishna, Bhagavad-Gita 15.14)

53. Do you know the time?

If you know the Time, then you accept Krishna, as Krishna is Time.

"The Supreme person [Krishna] said: I am time, the destroyer of the material creations, with the exception of you [the Pandavas]. I have come here to destroy all the warriors on both sides." (Lord Krishna, Bhagavad-Gita 11.32)

As each second passes, we get older, more diseased, closer to death, closer to our next body. No one can deny the existence of time (Krishna) and no one can stop time (Krishna). The sooner you accept Krishna, the sooner you will stop wasting your short and precious human birth.

54. Do you drink water in the light?

If you drink water in the light then you accept Krishna, as Krishna is the taste of water and the light of the sun.

"I am the taste of water, the light of the moon and sun, the syllable 'aum' in the Vedic scriptures, the sound vibration in ether, and the ability in man." (Lord Krishna, Bhagavad-Gita 7.8)

Every time you drink water, you should thank Krishna, as he is the taste of water. When you wake up in the morning, you should thank Krishna, as he is the light of the sun and in the evening he is the light of the moon. If you are able to do anything, then you should thank Krishna, as he is the ability in man.

55. Why is life full of ups and downs?

One time we are very happy and another time we are sad. This is the law of nature. We can't always be happy nor can we always be in distress. Just like the stock market, for some periods it goes up, for some periods it goes down, and sometimes it crashes.

Don't be disturbed when there is joy or sorrow in your life. They will come and go like the seasons. Instead, work towards ending this cycle of ups and downs.

"The winter and summer seasons will come and go. In a similar way, due to one's perception, happiness and distress will come and go. One should learn to tolerate them, without being disturbed." (Lord Krishna, Bhagavad-Gita 2.14)

56. Who are the Demigods?

The demigods are very powerful living beings who, live on the higher planets. They are more powerful than us but they are not God. They are like the vice presidents, and directors in a corporation. The CEO is Krishna and all others are the human beings like you and me.

Brahma is the vice president of creation. It's his job to create everything within the universe at the beginning of each cycle.

Shiva is the vice president of destruction. It's his job to destroy everything within this universe at the end of each cycle.

Indra is the director of the heavenly planets. Durga is the director of material energy and so on. In this way there are around 33 million demigods who perform various tasks in the universe. All the demigods report to Krishna directly or indirectly. Just like in a corporation, everyone reports to the CEO, either directly or indirectly.

57. How great are the Demigods?

When 8.64 billion years pass on Earth, one day passes for Brahma and his life span is 311 trillion years. He can walk on air, and water. He has created a whole universe with food; brought back the dead; traveled from one planet to another without any machine and so on.

There are millions of Brahmas, one in each universe. This universe we live in is the smallest one. There are other universes, which are millions of times bigger than this one.

Those with the mentality of a bacteria (most of us) will find the above hard to digest.

58. Should the Demigods be worshipped?

No. The demigods should be respected but not worshipped.

"One who knows me [Krishna] as the beneficiary of all sacrifices, penances, austerities, and the supreme Lord of all the planets, demigods, and the well-wisher of all living beings, can attain peace from the miseries of material life." (Lord Krishna, Bhagavad-Gita 5.29)

Krishna is the Lord of all the demigods and thus you should only worship Lord Krishna.

"Those who are less intelligent, worship the demigods. The results achieved by worshipping the demigods are temporary, and after this life they go to the planets of the demigods. My devotees go to my supreme planet." (Lord Krishna, Bhagavad-Gita 7.23)

Those who are less intelligent will worship the demigods and they will get limited and temporary benefits and at death they will go to the material planets of the demigods. On all the material planets, life is full of misery, old age, disease, and death. Those who worship Lord Krishna will go to his supreme planet, where one will get a beautiful body that is eternal, full of bliss, knowledge, and no misery.

59. Does Satan really exist?

No, when humans engage in violence against any living being, hatred, wickedness, lust, greed, anger, pride and so on, they have become Satanic. There is no species of living beings that are Satan, any human who engages in sin is called the Satan, until they stop the sinful activities.

Some people foolishly stone walls, as they think this will kill the Satan. They should stone themselves whenever they engage in sinful activities, this will really stop the Satanic values.

60. What are the four Yugas (Ages)?

There are four ages in which we keep circulating:

Satya Yuga: The age of truth. Only one religion (Sanatan Dharma) exists in the whole World. The Yuga lasts 1.728 million years.

Treta Yuga: The introduction of ignorance takes place in this age, but still only one religion exists in the whole World. The Yuga lasts 1.296 million years.

Dvapara Yuga: Decline in the truth and religious values takes effect in this age, but still only one religion is followed in the whole World. The Yuga lasts 864,000 years.

Kali Yuga: The age of darkness, ignorance, and degradation. Many man made religions and deviations mushroom in the World. The Yuga lasts 432,000 years.

We are currently 5000 years into Kali Yuga. As each day passes, man is becoming more ignorant and degraded. The result of which is more suffering for mankind.

"One day of Brahma lasts one thousand cycles of four yugas [4.32 billion years]. The night is also of the same duration. At the start of Brahma's day, all living beings become manifested from the un-manifest state. Then at night, all living beings become un-manifest again. This is repeated again, and again. At the beginning of each day of Brahma, all living beings are manifested, and at night, they are helplessly un-manifested." (Lord Krishna, Bhagavad-Gita 8.17-19)

61. Is Bollywood demonic?

Yes. The theme of most Bollywood movies is lust and materialism. By Vedic standards, a half-naked girl dancing silly on the street is called a prostitute. By watching Bollywood movies, you will slowly and unknowingly attain the demonic qualities that are portrayed in movies. These are meat eating, gambling, lust, greed, anger, materialism, and ignorance of spirituality.

The simple fact is that what you see and hear on TV, will eventually manifest in your home. This means lust, greed, anger, ignorance of spirituality and so on. You should not watch Bollywood movies, unless you want to degrade yourself, others, and move down in life (lower species).

62. Is America the Supreme Destination?

Most people in India and many other countries are crazy about America. They want to go to America and become American Citizens. What is the difference between life in India and America?

- There is old age in India and America.
- There is disease in India and America.
- The death rate in India and America is the same, 100%.
- Outside India there is more spiritual degradation.
- Most people in India know that we are the soul and those outside think we are the body (no spiritual knowledge).

The destination for all living beings should be the abode of God. Where you will get a beautiful body which is eternal, full of bliss, full of knowledge, no old age, no disease, no death, and there is no need to work.

For millions of years, India was pure and prosperous but now it has become degraded due to Indians becoming beggars of foreign cultures and technology, instead of being givers of India's greatest asset, spiritual knowledge.

"The supreme destination, which is infallible, the ultimate destination, a place from which, once having reached it, one never returns. That is my supreme abode." (Lord Krishna, Bhagavad-Gita 8.21)

A short life on the land of Bharat-varsa (India) is better than a lifetime on the planet of Brahmaloka, where the lifespan is trillions of years. Because after a long life on Brahmaloka, one must return to this or other planet and go through the repeated cycle of birth, old age, disease, misery, and death. In one short lifetime in India, if one can elevate his consciousness to Krishna consciousness, then the result will be that this will be the last material life. At death, the soul will be immediately transferred to the spiritual abode called Vaikuntha. There one can live in a beautiful body eternally, with no problems. Even the demigods, who are now living on the higher planets, wish to take birth in India when they end their current life. This is because outside India, there is godlessness.

63. Is a degree in medicine the king of Education?

Many parents are crazy about getting their children into medicine or other high earning material professions. They will ensure the children work hard at school and will spend all their accumulated wealth on their children's education. At the time of death, will the degree in Medicine help the parents or the children?

A student of medicine will study hundreds of books. Will the Bhagavad-Gita be one of those books?

At death, all our degrees are completely useless. Those who have some intelligence will study medicine or get some other high level education, and at the same time they will also gain some spiritual knowledge, by studying the Bhagavad-Gita and Srimad Bhagavatam. The result of this is that they will earn good money by practicing medicine or other high level professions and at death, because they gained some spiritual knowledge, they will get a chance to advance in spiritual life in their next life by being born in families who are engaged in devotional service. Then eventually they will be advanced enough in spiritual knowledge to go back to the spiritual creation called Vaikuntha, where everyone has a beautiful body that is eternal, full of bliss, and knowledge.

Those who are less intelligent will not be interested in gaining spiritual knowledge from the Bhagavad-Gita and will focus only on the material education, then at death because they have no spiritual knowledge, they will take birth in families who are in darkness, as they have no interest in spirituality. Those who are in darkness gradually sink into lower human species and eventually back into the animal and plant kingdoms.

"This is the purest knowledge, the king of education, the king of the most confidential knowledge. It is the highest knowledge, most righteous, and everlasting." (Lord Krishna, Bhagavad-Gita 9.2)

Krishna states that the Bhagavad-Gita is the king of education. This knowledge will eternally benefit you. Will your knowledge of medicine benefit you, life after life?

I am not saying don't study or don't become a doctor. My point is that will it hurt to add one more book (The Bhagavad-Gita) to the list of hundreds of books that a student will study?

64. What is the result of material education but no spiritual education?

By being very well materially educated, one has simply become a polished animal.

"At death, those who have developed the mode of goodness, will go to the higher planets where the saintly persons live. Those who have developed the mode of passion, will take birth among those engaged in materialistic activities. Those who have developed the mode of ignorance, will take birth in the animal kingdom."(Lord Krishna, Bhagavad-Gita 14.14-15)

The result of spiritual ignorance is that one falls down into the plant and animal kingdoms. At the end of this life, the souls of spiritually ignorant persons go through the evolutionary process of transmigration from one body to another. After going through 8 million species in the plant and animal kingdoms, the soul will once again get another human body, this takes around 52 billion years. This is the reason why human birth is so precious and thus we should not waste it on material development and spiritual degradation.

One should become materially educated to get a good job and earn money to pay the bills, but at the same time, one should get some spiritual education and engage in Bhakti Yoga to ensure the soul does not fall down into lower species after this life.

Charles Darwin and Albert Eienstein were both very well materially educated, but where are they now? Where are all those well educated people that you once new or came across? Do they now live eternally in the same body?

Did the material education help them to overcome birth, old age, disease, misery, and death? Does any University professor guarantee that by becoming well educated, one will be able to live in the same body eternally with no problems?

The thousands of Vedic saints like Swami Srila Prabhupada, guarantee that if one becomes well educated in the teachings of the Bhagavad-Gita, and practices it by performing Bhakti Yoga. Then at death, one will immediately be transferred to the spiritual creation where they will live in the same beautiful body eternally with no misery.

65. What is the caste system?

There is no caste system as the word 'caste' implies that which is fixed from birth and not changeable. But there is a Vedic class system, which is defined in the Bhagavad-Gita as follows:

"Brahmanas, ksatriyas, vaisyas, and sudras are determined by their nature, qualities, and work performed." (Lord Krishna, Bhagavad-Gita Original 18.41)

What this means is that based on the qualities developed by a person. A person will belong to one of four classes:

Brahmans - Peacefulness, self-control, austerity, purity, tolerance, honesty, knowledge, wisdom and religiousness. Those who possess these qualities should be the leaders in society.

Ksatriyas - Heroism, power, determination, resourcefulness, courage in battle, generosity and leadership. Those who possess these qualities should be the administrators in society.

Vaisyas - Farming, cow protection and business. Those who possess these qualities should be the business owners and farmers.

Sudras - Labor and service to others. Those who possess these qualities should work under the guidance of the above classes.

Every corporation in the World uses the Vedic class system. For example, in a corporation people are employed based on the qualities of work they have developed. Some are vice presidents, some are managers, some are admin clerks, and some are janitors.

It is a fact that everyone is not the same; this can be proven by the fact that not everyone has all the good qualities or all bad qualities. By following the Vedic class system, everyone will strive to become the best among men. Those at the top (Brahmans) will strive to keep their high position, and those below will strive to advance to a higher position. At work, do you want to advance or would you prefer to stay in the same position?

Everyone would agree that at work, there should be opportunities for advancement for everyone based on the effort put in by each worker. If there are no opportunities for advancement based on the efforts of the workers, then everyone loses the motivation to work and the quality of workers diminishes. This would result in the collapse of the corporation.

In a classless society, there is no motivation to develop good qualities and everyone becomes degraded into the lowest class. This is the case everywhere in the World today. The leaders in most countries around the World are thieves, liars, and have no spiritual knowledge. The result of this is that the public suffers with injustice, high taxes, inflation, unemployment, and insecurity.

Wouldn't it be nice if all the Politicians were peaceful, self-controlled, pure, tolerant, honest, knowledgeable, and religious? This is the aim of the Vedic class system. To ensure that suitably qualified personnel are appointed suitable roles in society. This concept is already used in corporations around the World.

The current caste system in India is a complete corruption of the Vedic class system that is prescribed by Krishna in the Bhagavad-Gita and so it should be rejected. Currently the son of a Brahman is also called a Brahman, even though the son only has the qualities of a Sudra. Can the son of a high court judge also be called a judge? Can the son of a doctor be also called a doctor? The simple answer is no. One can only be called a judge or doctor, if one has developed the qualities of a judge or doctor.

66. What is barbaric?

* The non-Hindus have a history of treating humans as slaves. The Hindus have never treated humans as slaves. Slavery is barbaric.
* Hatred towards Jews, Christians, Muslims, Atheists, and all others is barbaric. It's God who is creating the variety of people and thus those who have hatred towards anyone are the enemies of God.
* The non-Vedic scriptures define animals as food and thus their followers slaughter animals by the millions daily. Killing is barbaric.
* To divide humans into believers and unbelievers is barbaric.
* To kill in the name of God is barbaric.
* To take women captive is barbaric.
* To force anyone to follow a particular religion is barbaric.
* To have sex with children is barbaric.

"One who does not hate anyone; is friendly and compassionate to all living beings; shares his belongings with others; has no sense of ownership; free from ego; even-minded in both happiness and distress; forgiving; tolerant in all situations; always satisfied; worships me with determination and

devotion. Such a person is very dear to me." (Lord Krishna, Bhagavad-Gita 12.13-14)

67. What takes away the good qualities in a person?

Bad association and wrong knowledge takes away the good qualities in a person. When we are born, we have pure thoughts. A child doesn't see any difference between White, Asian, and Black people. Everyone is fun to play with and there is no such thing as money. Everything belongs to everyone. But as the child grows up, due to the association with adults, the child slowly develops a mentality of likes and dislikes towards people and things. Parents and relatives condition the children.

Modern lifestyle of partying, discoing (western culture), irreligious values (envy and hatred), Bollywood movies, and ignorance (lack of knowledge and misunderstanding) slowly and unknowingly drain away the righteous qualities in a person.

"Just as the wind can carry away a boat on the water. The mind that gives in to one of the roaming senses, can carry away the intelligence of a person." (Lord Krishna, Bhagavad-Gita 2.67)

"By thinking about sense objects, a person develops attachment to the objects, and from attachment, desires develop. When the desires are not fulfilled, anger develops. From anger, arises delusion, from delusion there is confusion and loss of reasoning. This results is loss of intelligence, and when intelligence is lost, one falls down into lower species." (Lord Krishna, Bhagavad-Gita 2.62-63)

68. How do I achieve peace of mind?

Don't satisfy your desires.

Every day we desire to buy this and that, go here and there, and do this and that and so on. We must realize that satisfying our desires today will only result in more desires tomorrow. So try to stop satisfying your desires by saying no you don't need that, you don't need to go there, you can live without it and so on.

"The ocean is always being filled by waters from different rivers, but still it remains steady. Like-wise, a person who is not disturbed by the constant flow of desires can achieve peace, and not the person who fulfills all his desires. A person,

who gives up all desires, ego, and sense of ownership, can alone achieve peace." (Lord Krishna, Bhagavad-Gita 2.70-71)

A person says 'I want peace'. If you remove the 'I' (ego), and the 'want' (desires). Then you will be left with 'peace'.

69. How do I become happy?

The bad news is that, only those who are in complete ignorance or those who are completely wise can be happy in the material creation. The others cannot always be happy.

The good news is that we can make this our last material life and go back to the spiritual creation, Vaikuntha. There we can live in the same beautiful body eternally, with complete happiness, full of bliss, full of knowledge, and no trace of anxiety. One who practices Bhakti Yoga can achieve this.

"The great souls, who have achieved perfection, attain me [Krishna]. They do not take birth again in this material creation, which is temporary and full of miseries." (Lord Krishna, Bhagavad-Gita 8.15)

In our short lives, before going back to the spiritual creation, we can minimize our suffering by being satisfied with whatever we have and not being disturbed by what others have or say. Don't be disturbed by whatever good or bad that happens to you or others.

"If one can tolerate the urges of desires and anger, he can become happy in this life." (Lord Krishna, Bhagavad-Gita 5.23)

70. Is life on all planets miserable?

Many people believe that if they go to heaven, they will be happy. But this is not the case. Those who go to the heavenly planets will enjoy heavenly delights but they also grow old, become diseased, and die one day. Then they come back down to Earth or other similar planet, and will again have to go through the pains in the womb, baby life (crying), infant life (wanting candies and toys, none of which will satisfy), teenage life (acne and stress of education), adulthood (marital problems and working stress), old age, disease, and death. Then go through the whole thing again and again.

The only way out is to go back to the spiritual creation called Vaikuntha. This can only be achieved by developing the good qualities listed below and Bhakti Yoga. On the spiritual planets, people live in beautiful bodies that are eternal, full of bliss, full of knowledge, no terrorism, no marital problems, no taxes, no violence, no thieves, no liars, no cheaters, no corruption, no hatred, and so on.

"Everyone on the lowest planet to the highest planet of Brahmaloka, in the material creation is subjected to the miseries of repeated birth and death. But those who attain me [Krishna], never take birth again." (Lord Krishna, Bhagavad-Gita 8.16)

71. What are the three modes of material nature?

One is always forced to act in one of three modes of material nature, goodness, passion and ignorance. These modes compete in exerting their influence upon us.

"Goodness, passion, and ignorance are the three modes of material nature. The qualities developed by a person are based on these three modes." (Lord Krishna, Bhagavad-Gita 14.5)

The Mode of Goodness - A person in the mode of goodness is free from all sinful reactions and is in a condition of happiness and knowledge. One who dies in the mode of goodness attains the higher planets.

"The mode of goodness is purity. This mode illuminates and frees one from sinful reactions. Those situated in this mode become inclined to happiness, spiritual knowledge, and pure thoughts." (Lord Krishna, Bhagavad-Gita 14.6)

The Mode of Passion - A person in the mode of passion is plagued by unlimited desires for material enjoyment, greed and lust (especially sexual pleasures). To satisfy these desires, one is always forced to engage in hard work that binds the person to sinful reactions, resulting in misery. A person in this mode is never satisfied with the position already acquired. One, who dies in the mode of passion, takes birth again on planets like Earth among persons who are full of desires, greed and lust.

"The mode of passion is intense craving for sense gratification. This mode creates desires and lust. Those situated in this mode become bound to materialistic activities." (Lord Krishna, Bhagavad-Gita 14.7)

The Mode of Ignorance - A person in the mode of ignorance is in delusion. It fosters laziness, foolishness and madness. One who dies in the mode of ignorance takes birth in the animal kingdom or on the hellish planets.

"The mode of ignorance is darkness or delusion. This mode creates carelessness, madness, and laziness. Those situated in this mode become degraded." (Lord Krishna, Bhagavad-Gita 14.8)

By understanding that the three modes are active and not you (the soul) and by realizing that you are separate from the modes of nature, the influence of material nature on you will gradually diminish.

72. Should we be kind and tolerant like a tree?

The trees stand in the cold and heat. They give fruits, vegetables, and shade to all living beings. They don't discriminate against any living being. Whether they get little water or no water, they will still try to provide for all. We should become tolerant and kind like the trees.

Don't kill trees, plant more trees in your gardens.

73. How can I go to the kingdom of God?

Give up all sinful activities like meat eating, gambling, drinking, smoking/chewing tobacco, partying, discoing, and boyfriend/girlfriend. Realize that there is only one God, and be friendly to all living beings. This mentality will lead you to the kingdom of God.

"By pure devotional service unto me [Krishna], one can know me as the Supreme person in truth, and thereafter one can enter into my kingdom." (Lord Krishna, Bhagavad-Gita 18.55)

74. Is your mind your friend or your enemy?

The mind is always flickering and agitating. When it is controlled, it becomes the friend of the soul, and when it is not controlled, it becomes the enemy of the soul. How many times have you had two opposite thoughts about doing something? This is the mind and the soul or super soul.

"The mind is a friend to those who have control over it, and the mind is the enemy for those who do not control it." (Lord Krishna, Bhagavad-Gita 6.6)

75. What are the moral values of civilized humans?

- Be kind to all living beings.
- Be sociable. Visit your friends and relatives often.
- Don't eat your brothers and sisters (Vegetarian).
- Share all your belongings with others.
- Consider yourself to be the lowest (Free from ego and pride).
- Treat others well whether you are in distress or happiness.
- Be very tolerant in all situations.
- Always be satisfied with whatever you get/don't get.
- Always control yourself.
- Don't be fussy with food. Eat whatever is available, provided its vegetarian.
- Don't be a miser.
- Give up sense of ownership.
- Be clean. Take bath at least once a day, brush teeth at least twice a day, and keep the home and work area clean.
- Never lie, always tell the truth.
- Never cheat or mislead anyone.
- Never gamble.
- Never drink alcohol or take drugs.
- Never smoke or chew tobacco.
- Be free from lust. If you are a man: All women older than you are your elder sisters or mothers. All women younger than you are your sisters or daughters. If you are a woman: All men older than you are your fathers or elder brothers. All men younger than you are your brothers or sons.
- Don't behave like the dogs on the street. No boyfriend/girlfriend.
- Always help others according to your ability.
- Always be charitable according to your capacity.
- Always be concerned for the welfare and wellness of others.
- Accept that you are responsible for your own bills (Karma).
- Accept that you are the soul, which is eternal (Reincarnation).

One should follow and recite this list of good qualities at least once a week, to become purified and elevated to higher consciousness.

"Absence of fear; purity of heart; charitable; striving for spiritual knowledge by studying the Vedic scriptures; lives a simple life; always straight forward in his dealings; always truthful; not violent; free from anger; not greedy; always gentle; forgiving; very clean; not envious of others; compassionate to all living beings; doesn't talk non-sense; has no pride; doesn't mislead others – These are some of the qualities of those with divine nature." (Lord Krishna, Bhagavad-Gita 16.1-3)

76. Should we only eat fresh food?

Yes, we should try to only eat freshly cooked foods. Processed, frozen, micro waved food, and meat is dear to those in darkness.

"People in the mode of ignorance like to eat foods that are prepared more than three hours before eating. Foods that have a bad smell [eggs], decomposed [meat], tasteless, and stale." (Lord Krishna, Bhagavad-Gita 17.10)

77. Are wholesome foods good for us?

Yes.

"People in the mode of goodness like to eat foods that are juicy, fatty, and nutritious. These foods give strength, health, happiness, and increase duration of life." (Lord Krishna, Bhagavad-Gita 17.8)

78. Are hot and salty foods bad for us?

Yes.

"People in the mode of passion like to eat foods that are bitter, sour, salty, very hot, pungent, dry, and burning. These foods cause disease, distress, and misery." (Lord Krishna, Bhagavad-Gita 17.9)

79. Are same sex relationships wrong?

Yes. But we should help people of such inclinations advance in spirituality and not hate them or give them a hard time.

80. What is Bhakti Yoga?

There are many types of yoga systems, the yoga system described and recommended in the Bhagavad-Gita is Bhakti Yoga. This means to link with Krishna (God) or devotional service unto God:

- Become pure hearted. This can be accomplished by developing all the good qualities that are described in question 75.
- Offer all foods that you cook first to Krishna then you can eat them (parsadam). Krishna will not accept meat, fish, eggs, onions, and garlic. The food must also be freshly cooked (less than 3 hours).
- Chant the maha mantra:

**Hare Krishna, Hare Krishna,
Krishna Krishna, Hare Hare,
Hare Rama, Hare Rama,
Rama Rama, Hare Hare**

- Offer flowers and Tulsi leaves to Krishna daily. This requires planting of flower bearing (especially roses) and Tulsi plants in your gardens.
- Perform deity worship of Radha and Krishna daily.
- Engage in some service at your local temple.
- Read the Vedic scriptures, especially the Bhagavad-Gita and Srimad Bhagavatam.
- Preach all the above to others. Preaching is the highest devotional service unto Lord Krishna.

The above devotional service activities should be performed according to your capacity and ability, but do as much as you can and the result will be that this will be your last miserable material life. At death, you (the soul) will be immediately transferred to the spiritual creation, where you will live in the same beautiful body eternally on the same planet as Lord Narayan, an expansion of Lord Krishna, or on the planet of Lord Krishna himself.

"The great souls bow down to me [Krishna], worship me, and always chant my names and glories, with determination and devotion." (Lord Krishna, Bhagavad-Gita 9.14)

"Just become my devotee, always think of me, bow down to me, and worship me. Then you will come to me, without fail. I promise you this, as you are very dear to me." (Lord Krishna, Bhagavad-Gita 18.65)

"If one who is devoted to me, teaches this supreme secret to other devotees, he shall be performing the highest devotional service unto me, and he will certainly come back to me. There is no other servant on Earth, who is more dear to me." (Lord Krishna, Bhagavad-Gita 18.68-69)

A Bhakti Yogi is one who has given up desires for material possessions and all his activities are done only for the satisfaction of the supreme (Linked to the Supreme).

81. What is human and animal consciousness?

The difference between human and animal consciousness is that humans are inquisitive and considerate.

Real human beings enquire:

- Who am I, and where have I come from?
- Where was I before this life?
- Where will I be after this life?
- Who exactly is God?
- Why do I suffer?
- Why is everyone born in different situations?

Animals do not enquire. They simply eat, sleep, mate, and defend.

Humans are compassionate, they always think of others. The animals mind their own business and don't think of others.

The humans are charitable, the animals are not charitable. They simply enjoy everything for themselves. The humans can be friendly to all living beings. The animals eat other animals, and are often aggressive. The animals like donkeys are busy working hard all day. The humans also have to work hard to make a living, but at the same time they think of what is ahead after this life. The donkeys don't think of what is ahead.

Do you have human or animal consciousness?

82. Can you describe God?

I asked many people (non-Hindus) this question and I got the following replies:

God cannot be seen (invisible).
God is love.
God is in the sky.
God has not been seen by anyone.
God was crucified.

None of these people have actually answered the question. They obviously have not read the Bhagavad-Gita. Just by looking at the Bhagavad-Gita for one second, you can see the all-beautiful God. By reading a few pages, you will know how merciful, loving, and great, God is. In the Srimad Bhagavatam, full description and history of God is given.

- His complexion is dark-blue, like that of a rain filled cloud.
- His eyes are like lotus petals.
- He is ever youthful.
- He is full of bliss
- His beauty excels that of thousands of cupids.
- He likes to play the flute.
- He wears a peacock feather in his crown.
- He wears the Kaustubha jewel around his neck.
- He wears yellow garments.

If you know God's name, address, description, his qualities, pastimes he performed, the history of when he appeared in the past, when he will appear in the future, how he maintains, how he witnesses all our actions; then you know God, otherwise you don't know. You will find all this information, only in the Vedic scriptures like the Bhagavad-Gita and the Srimad Bhagavatam.

Lord Krishna in his original form

83. What keeps people in ignorance?

Not being open minded, lack of proper knowledge and understanding, keeps people in ignorance. Arjuna acquired the knowledge of the Bhagavad-Gita to overcome his confused state. When Maharaj Pariksit was told he had 7 days to live, he acquired the knowledge of the Srimad Bhagavatam to make his consciousness pure before his death.

By singing or listening to bhajans is not going to teach you what is right and what is wrong. It's the right knowledge that will make your consciousness pure.

"Just as a blazing fire turns firewood to ashes. Knowledge burns all reactions to material actions." (Lord Krishna, Bhagavad-Gita 4.37)

All negative qualities, such as lust, anger, violence, hatred, and greed, are nothing but a manifestation of ignorance.

The difference between a good doctor and an average one is that the good doctor will have more knowledge and understanding. The good doctor can be used, whereas the average doctor is useless.

84. What makes people engage in sinful activities?

Ignorance and evil ideology causes people to engage in sinful activities like killing (animals or humans), violence, drinking, gambling, and hatred.

85. What is foolishness?

When one considers anything based on his/her own knowledge, ability, and perception. This is called foolishness.

Some people say no one has seen God. Have you seen what the 6.5 billion people in the World today or the trillions of people who lived in the past have seen? No! So how can you say no one has seen God?

Some people say we have a form and we are not great, and so God cannot have a form, as he is great. You have a form and you are not a brain surgeon, does this mean that all brain surgeons must be formless?

Some people say we suffer because God is not present everywhere, to help us. Just because you can't be everywhere, does it mean that God can't be everywhere?

Some say, people are born unfortunate in their only life so that they will be judged earlier than others. First of all, when is the Day of Judgment? No answer. Who would choose to be born blind in their only life, so they can be judged earlier?

Some people say if a person produces a small chunk of gold in his hand, then he must be God. What about the person who has created the gold mines?

Some people say their God will save them on the Day of Judgment, and until then they have to suffer. Will you work for a company that will pay you on the Day of Judgment?

Some people believe that God only has one son. Even pigs have many sons, so why should the almighty God only have one son?

"The foolish persons cannot understand how a living entity quits one body to take another. But those with knowledge can see this." (Lord Krishna, Bhagavad-Gita 15.10)

"Foolish men, disregard me when I appear in a human like body. They do not know that my nature is supreme, and I am the great Lord of everything." (Lord Krishna, Bhagavad-Gita 9.11)

86. What are the problems of material life?

Your partner may be cheating you.
The contractor may be cheating you.
Your marriage may end at any time.
You may lose your job at any time.
Your business may go down at any time.
You may be kicked out of your house at any time.
Your savings will run out at any time.
Your retirement savings may become worthless.
You may develop a serious disease like cancer at any time.
Your children may become diseased at any time.
Your loved one may die at any time.

Suffering is caused by nature in the form of natural disasters like flooding, earthquakes, droughts, crop failures, and so on.

Others cause suffering, like your relatives, friends, and family members.

Suffering is caused by personal relationship with others, like marital problems, and work/business relationships and so on.

87. What are the daily decisions we have to make?

Every day we are faced with decisions to make in our life.

Shall I do this or do that?
Will he/she be ok?
Shall I buy now or wait?
How much shall I spend?
When will I do it?
When will I go?
Which should I choose?
Who should I choose?
When will I retire?
Will it work out?

Based on our knowledge, tolerance level, material intelligence, and spiritual intelligence. We will make the right choice or the wrong choice. For which we will suffer or enjoy in the future. One day we will make someone suffer and another day it will be our turn to suffer.

Many times we will be placed in a trance and forced to act in ignorance.

The above list of decisions and problems are real and affects everyone. By knowing these possible situations in advance will help you to avoid some of them, and help you get through the others with minimum misery.

"The five factors of action are: The physical body; Modes of material nature; the various senses; various efforts; The Supreme. These are the five factors, which cause whatever right or wrong action, a person performs by his body, thought, and speech." (Lord Krishna, Bhagavad-Gita 18.14-15)

As stated above, things will happen to us based on our own efforts and sometimes by the will of God. This means that failure or rejection is many times the will of God for our own good.

88. What is karma?

For every action you take, there will be a reaction in the future. You are responsible for all your actions. You have to pay your own bills. This is the law of karma.

Whatever activity we do, good or bad, brings us good or bad reactions. For every action you take, you will face a reaction in the future, which could be a few seconds away or 20 years away or your next incarnation. If you take good actions, you will face good reactions. This may come in the form of good health, wealth or birth on higher planets etc. If you take bad actions, you will face bad reactions in the future. The bad reactions may come in the form of disease, poverty or birth on one of the hellish planets etc.

"Actions taken in the mode of goodness are purifying and result in piousness. Actions taken in the mode of passion result in misery, and actions taken in the mode of ignorance, result in degradation." (Lord Krishna, Bhagavad-Gita 14.16)

89. Why do we suffer?

When we suffer, we are facing the reactions to the bad actions we took in our past.

Our actions include everything we do, including our physical deeds, our words and thoughts. There will be a reaction to all our actions.

Taking good actions builds our good karma (joy and happiness in the future).

Taking bad actions builds our bad karma (disease and suffering in the future).

Actions, which result in bad Karma: Eating meat, violence, hatred, ignorance, harshness, untruthfulness, lust, anger, greed, attachments, desires, gambling, ego, and alcohol.

Actions, which build good Karma: Vegetarianism, non-violence, generosity, charity, self-control, truthfulness, simplicity, forgiveness, religiousness, cleanliness, free from attachment, desires, and ego.

The reason why some people suffer more than others is that they sinned more than others in their past and thus they are now facing the bad reactions to the bad actions taken in their past.

90. Why do good people suffer?

The reason why some good people suffer is because, although they are now good, they are facing the reactions to the bad actions they took in their past. But because they are now taking good actions, they will face good reactions (be happy) in the future.

91. Why bad people don't suffer?

The reason why some really rotten people enjoy a good life despite being rotten, is that they are now facing the reactions to the good actions they took in their past. However, because they are taking bad actions now (being rotten), they will face bad reactions in the future (suffer).

God does not make one happy for no reason nor does God make one suffer for no reason. Karma is a very just law.

92. Are those who live in big houses very fortunate?

Not all of them.

Those who live in small houses may think that those who live in big houses are very fortunate. But this is not always the case. Many of those who live in big houses have more stress, diseases, and personal problems, compared to those who live in smaller houses.

Which would you choose: Live in a big house and suffer from cancer or live in a small house with no cancer?

Which would you choose: Live in a big house with marital problems or live in a small house with no marital problems?

Some may actually be living in a small house with cancer and marital problems. But there are also people living in a big house with cancer and marital problems.

We should realize that our current situation is due to our own doing (past actions) and thus accept it without comparing ourselves with others. If one can control the constant flow of desires and be satisfied with whatever one has, then peace of mind will follow.

"If one can tolerate the urges of desires and anger, he can become happy in this life." (Lord Krishna, Bhagavad-Gita 5.23)

93. How do we minimize the reactions to our actions?

"Just as a lotus leaf is in the water but it's not touched by the water, perform your work without being attached to the results, and offer the results to me [Krishna]. In this way, you will not incur sins or face bad reactions." (Lord Krishna, Bhagavad-Gita 5.10)

If you use some of the money you earn, in serving humanity and Krishna, this is proof that you are not attached to the results of your work, and you are offering the results (some money) to Krishna. In this way, you will not face any karmic reactions caused by your work.

"Do your duty without considering happiness or distress, profit or loss, victory or defeat. In this way, you will never face bad reactions." (Lord Krishna, Bhagavad-Gita 2.38)

In a sports match, if you are attached to seeing your team, win. Then if they lose, you will be upset for many days. This is the reaction to being attached to a win result. But if you were not attached to any result, then you will not be affected by the result. You will be able to accept a loss or win without getting upset.

Many parents desire for their children to become doctors and in many cases, they do become doctors. But the parents then face the bad reactions for having being attached to the results of their son's education. They have problems in the form of not getting along with their doctor son or health or other problems. The parents should send their children to school, but not desire for any results. In this way, there will be no bad reactions.

94. What are the symptoms of a spiritual master?

* He can answer the question 'Who is God the person?"
* He can give details on the description, history, past times, and opulence of God.
* He will be completely non-violent and peaceful to all living beings. This means he should not be engaged in killing animals or humans. Thus he should be a pure vegetarian and not engaged in wars.
* He is simple, tolerant, truthful, forgiving, and merciful.
* He is not lusty.
* He will teach how to serve God.
* He will quote from the Vedic scriptures to back up his statements.

"The symptoms of a sadhu are that he is tolerant, peaceful, merciful, pure hearted, friendly to all living beings, and he follows the scriptures." (Srimad Bhagavatam 3.25.21)

Now days there are many bogus Gurus and Swamis who preach their own non-sense philosophy and completely deviate from the teachings of the Vedic scriptures. So be aware of this and only accept the teachings of someone if they can back up their statements by quoting from the Vedic scriptures. Throughout this book, I have quoted verses from the Bhagavad-Gita to back up my statements.

"You can get true knowledge and understanding by serving and inquiring from a self-realized spiritual master who has seen the truth." (Lord Krishna, Bhagavad-Gita 4.34)

I would recommend his divine grace A.C. Bhaktivedanta Swami Prabhupada and his disciples. Visit www.Krishna.com for more information and visit an ISKCON temple near you.

95. Are women lower than men?

No, women are actually higher than men.

From a spiritual point of view, all living beings are unique individuals, all equal, full of bliss, full of knowledge and eternal.

We say Radha Krishna and not Krishna Radha. Radha is a woman and her name has to be addressed first, even before the Supreme person, Lord Krishna. We also say Sita Ram and not Ram Sita, Laxmi Narayan and not Narayan Laxmi.

The highest position that any living being can attain in the material and spiritual creations is that of gopis, they are women. The Gopis are the top most devotees of Lord Krishna.

"I am death, and the origin of all future living beings. Of the females, I am fame, beauty, pleasant speech, memory, intelligence, commitment, and patience." (Lord Krishna, Bhagavad-Gita 10.34)

When I compare myself with my wife, I have to agree with the above statements made by Lord Krishna. My wife has more friends than me, she is more beautiful than me, she talks better than me, she has more memory than me, she is more committed than me, and I have no patience.

96. Why should women be protected from degradation?

The women produce children, and they should teach them what is right, and what is wrong (religious principles). But when women become polluted, they become irreligious and the whole generation becomes degraded. For this reason, women should be protected from becoming polluted. Thus girls should not live away from the home and should be married off at an early age, 18-22. Otherwise the chances of them becoming polluted are very high. Unfortunately, now days, girls everywhere are rejecting culture and religion, and wanting what they call freedom. That is defined as partying, drinking, no culture, no religion, no respect for the elders, and behaving like the dogs on the street (boyfriends). This behavior is called animalism and after this rare human birth, these 2-legged animals will become 4-legged animals.

97. What is the result of not following the scriptures?

"Those who act according to their own whims, disregarding the regulations prescribed in the scriptures, never attain perfection, or happiness, or the supreme abode." (Lord Krishna, Bhagavad-Gita 16.23)

Those living beings who have no interest in culture, religion, and who do not follow any regulations as prescribed in the scriptures are called animals.

98. How great are some Yogis?

There are millions of yogis who can walk on water, and air; make themselves lighter than a cotton swab; travel from one planet to another, one universe to another; create planets and universes; multiply food; cure the sick, fly without any machine, and so on. The master of all yogis and mystic powers is called Yogeshwar (Krishna).

99. Why should you be charitable?

Donating money gives one the opportunity to become free from material attachments and thus material life. Those who do not donate simply waste the money on material possessions and become attached to a materialist life thus becoming bonded to material life for many lifetimes.

A foolish person works hard all his life, accumulating a big bank balance, properties, jewelry, fast cars, and other material possessions. Then he quits his body to take another, leaving behind everything.

Because he spent the money on himself and did not offer the results of his work (money) to God, he lived in sin and his next body will be that of a beggar.

A wise person spends his hard earned money on himself and gives a portion of it in charity. Thus when he quits his body, he will be able to enjoy his wealth in his next body too. He will be born in a rich family.

Did you ever wonder why some are born in rich families and some in poor families? Now you know why.

100. What is the best charity?

The giving of the gift of spiritual knowledge to your friends, relatives, and others is the best charity. The best welfare is to help others discover their real nature, spiritual self-realization.

The gifting of material goods only increases sense gratification and bondage to material life. Spiritual knowledge helps people to stop the sinful activities in their lives. This sets one free from material life, which is a cycle of birth, old age, disease, misery, and death.

101. What is the highest service to God?

All living beings are the children of God and thus anyone who helps God's children go back to their original abode, back to the spiritual creation, are most dear to God.

"If one who is devoted to me, teaches this supreme secret to other devotees, he shall be performing the highest devotional service unto me, and he will certainly come back to me. There is no other servant on Earth, who is more dear to me." (Lord Krishna, Bhagavad-Gita 18.68-69)

In this verse, Krishna states that if one teaches the Bhagavad-Gita to others, then that person is very dear to Krishna. Every devotee has the right to explain the Bhagavad-Gita according to his/her understanding to others. There are many who foolishly think that only a Sanyasi can explain the Bhagavad-Gita to others. Krishna very clearly states in this verse that anyone who is devoted to him can preach according to his/her ability and understanding. Lord Chaitanya, who is an incarnation of Lord Krishna, confirmed this by stating that anyone who is devoted to Lord Krishna should become a spiritual Guru.

This is Kali Yuga, the age of darkness, ignorance, and irreligion. The Bhagavad-Gita can save humanity, it's the only scripture that is spoken by God in person and also written by God in person.

Lord Krishna is the speaker of the Bhagavad-Gita and Ved Vasya who is an incarnation of Lord Krishna is the recorder of the Bhagavad-Gita and all other Vedic scriptures.

Until 5000 years ago, the whole world was called Bharat (the light), and there was only one religion in the whole world, Sanatan Dharma. But because of the influence of Kali Yuga, now the whole world is in darkness due to the irreligious principles of man-made teachings. These irreligious principles being; meat eating, God being unknown, we are the body (reject reincarnation), killing for virgins and wine in heaven, and so on. Only those who have the higher spiritual consciousness can bring light to the whole world again.

Out of the 6.5 billion people in the world, at least 5.5 billion are in complete ignorance as they are all godless. They cannot answer the simplest question 'Who is the Supreme person'? Only the Bhagavad-Gita answers this basic question. Lord Krishna is the supreme person (God).

102. What is the difference devotees and yogis?

Yogis are those who are only interested in their own advancement, they have no interest in helping others to advance. Devotees are those who help others to advance, they don't think about their own advancement.

Basically devotees, want to save others and yogis only care about themselves. Arjuna was a pure devotee and thus we should become pure devotees and not pure yogis, verses 18.68-69 confirm this.

103. Why no intoxications?

* Health – Alcohol and drugs are bad for the health.

* Suffering – Women and children suffer as the man of the house who drinks loses consciousness when drunk and engages in violence towards the wife and children, besides exposing them to exploitation by others.

* Financial ruin – Drugs and alcohol are not cheap and often, poor families suffer complete financial ruin due to the man of the house being addicted to alcohol or drugs.

* Addictive - Addiction results in extreme dependence on and attachment to the intoxicant. People become addicted to alcohol and drugs and in many cases this results in violence as the addicts will kill or steal to get hold of drugs or alcohol.

104. Why no gambling?

Gambling destroys the financial well being of families and causes suffering, mostly to women and children. Gamblers should realize that they would eventually be the losers.

105. Why no meat eating?

* Health – Scientific research has concluded that meat eaters are much more likely to suffer from cancer, heart disease, and other diseases than vegetarians.

* Morality – The cow gives her milk to people all her life, and then people kill and eat her. This is evil.

* Economics - It would take at least 20lbs of grains, many gallons of water, and some time to create just 1 lb of meat. Why not just take the 20 lbs of grains? This will feed 20 times more people than the 1 lb of meat. If everyone a vegetarian, there would be no poverty in the World.

* Environmental – The breeding and killing of animals for food is leading to the destruction of forests and global warming.

* Violence – The root cause of terrorism is evil ideology and mentality of violence. The mentality of violence is created when humans kill for a living. The simple fact is that a person who cuts the throats of animals is much more likely to cut the throats of humans too.

106. Why no Illicit sex?

Sex before marriage or outside marriage or attachment to sex is called illicit sex.

The governments around the World are very foolish by thinking that by promoting condoms they will stop AIDS. The only way to stop AIDS is for humans to stop behaving like the dogs on the street.

In this age, relationships and marriages are mostly based on sex impulses alone. This can be proven by the fact that most marriages end in a divorce. It is the children that suffer the most, all due to the lusty parents. Marriages often end due to one or both the partners wanting to move onto another mate. Just like the dogs on the street. Sexual lust only leads to misery in the long term, and binds one to material life for millions of lifetimes.

107. What is the mentality of those who don't follow the Bhagavad-Gita?

* Narrow-minded – They think their way is the only way and all others go to hell for simply being different.
* No faith in God – They cannot understand that God is in full control and thus it's God who is creating and maintaining all others.
* God is not real – God is either invisible or not known.
* Hatred – They cannot understand the concept of universal brotherhood.
* Animals – The animals are just food. Millions of animals are breed for food and killed daily.
* Who are we – They think they are the body.
* No eternality – They think this is the only life and thus we are not eternal.
* Purpose of religion – Some believe that by following their religion, they will go to heaven and enjoy sex and wine.
* No Karma – People suffer or enjoy by chance.

The result of above mentality is that we have hatred, more diseases, terrorism, poverty, wickedness, selfishness, godlessness, and destruction of nature.

108. Does Krishna curse those who don't follow him?

A man made God may curse those who don't follow him to a life in hell and he may be jealous, because he is not in control. But Krishna is not like this. Krishna is nice and he is in full control. He doesn't force anyone to follow him nor does he send anyone to hell just because they don't follow him.

"I have explained to you the most confidential knowledge. Now, think about it and then do as you wish." (Lord Krishna, Bhagavad-Gita 18.63)

After speaking the Bhagavad-Gita to Arjuna, Krishna gives him free will. He doesn't say Arjuna will go to hell if he doesn't follow him nor does Krishna say he will be jealous if Arjuna doesn't follow him. This is because Krishna is a mature and responsible person. Krishna is all loving and all merciful, the real God.

109. What is the mentality of those who follow the Bhagavad-Gita?

The devotees of Lord Krishna have the following mentality:

* Broad minded – They never say or think others will go to hell simply for being different.
* Full faith in Krishna – They know that God is in full control and thus don't have any problems with others.
* God is real – God is visible and known.
* Universal brotherhood - Consider all living beings as brothers and sisters. All living beings are the children of the one God and thus brothers and sisters.
* Animals – They are our brothers and sisters too. Thus no meat eating (vegetarianism).
* Who are we – We are not this body but the soul.
* Eternality – We are eternal and thus this is not the only life.
* Purpose of religion – A sincere devotee of Krishna only wants to eternally serve Krishna and has no desire for sense gratification. Thus no lust, no intoxications, no killing, and no speculation.
* Karma – People suffer or enjoy based on their past actions. Nothing happens by chance. As you sow, so shall you reap.

People with the above mentality make the World a safer, and peaceful place to live. Also, at the end of this life, these souls will go back to the spiritual creation and live eternally in the same beautiful body with God. A self-realized person has the above mentality.

"Being freed from attachments, fear, anger, and fully situated in thought of me, many have become purified by penance and knowledge of me. They all attained pure love for me. (Lord Krishna, Bhagavad-Gita 4.10)

110. What is a self-realized person?

* A person who realizes that he is not the material body but the soul.

    The material body is temporary but the soul is eternal, and one who knows this realizes that he (the soul) has been transmigrating from one body to another for countless lifetimes and thus his current body is just one of the millions of bodies he (the soul) has occupied. This means he is not the body but the soul within the body.

* A person who realizes his relationship with the supreme.

   The relationship between the living entities and the supreme (God), is that all living entities are part and parcel of the supreme. The means the qualities of all living entities (souls) are the same as those of the supreme. These qualities being eternality, blissfulness, and knowledge.

* A person who realizes that the part is meant to serve the whole.

   Just as the hand serves the body, the living entities who are part of the supreme, must serve the whole, thus serve the supreme.

* A person who has given up desires for material possessions and all his activities are done only for the satisfaction of the supreme.

* A person who teaches all the above to others.

   A self-realized person is concerned for the welfare of all living beings and thus wants to deliver all living beings back to the spiritual creation, where everyone is happy eternally.

"The great souls, who have achieved perfection, attain me [Krishna]. They do not take birth again in this material creation, which is temporary and full of miseries." (Lord Krishna, Bhagavad-Gita 8.15)

111. What is the result of being Krishna conscious?

The benefits of Krishna consciousness to the World are as follows:

* Non-violence – Krishna conscious people are totally non-violent. No killing (vegetarian).

* Simple people – Krishna conscious people believe in living a simple life (not materialistic).

* No druggies or drunkards – Krishna conscious people are not intoxicated. No drugs or alcohol.

* No hatred – Krishna conscious people believe God is the father of all living beings and thus we are all brothers and sisters.

* No Gamblers – Krishna conscious people don't gamble.

* Treat all people equally and nicely – Krishna conscious people view all living beings as souls and not physical bodies. Thus there are no

bodily designations; even the plants and animals are treated like human beings.

If you are serious about stopping terrorism, drugs, hatred, global warming, and AIDS, then become Krishna conscious and promote it.

112. Who should I follow?

People argue over who God is. First of all, know what qualities the applicant for the supreme position should have. These qualities are listed in question 7. Then compare the pastimes, miracles performed, and statements made by the applicants for the supreme position, and then there will be no doubt who is God and who isn't.

* Krishna lifted a mountain (Govardhana hill) for 7 days. Do you know anyone else who has lifted a mountain?

* Krishna expanded his body into 16108 forms. Do you know anyone else who can multiply himself into thousands of identical bodies or even once?

* Krishna swallowed a forest fire to save his friends. Do you know anyone else who has saved his followers in their current life?

* Krishna cured the diseased, including transforming a hunchback woman into a most beautiful woman. Do you know anyone else who has transformed the ugly into beautiful in their current life?

* Krishna brought the dead back to life. Do you know anyone else who has brought back the dead?

* Krishna defeated all those who challenged him including Kamsa, Putana, Bakasura, Kesi, Aghasura, and Sisupala. Do you know anyone else who has defeated all those who challenged him?

* Krishna saved all his followers in this life. Do you know anyone else who has saved all his followers in their current life?

* Krishna transformed himself into others. Do you know anyone else who can transform themselves into others?

* Krishna was born fully clothed. Do you know anyone else born clothed?

* Krishna has appeared in the same body more than 17,939 times in the current cycle alone. Do you know anyone else who has appeared with the same body this many times or even twice?

* Krishna never looks older than about 16. He is forever youthful, forever beautiful. Do you know anyone else who always looks youthful and beautiful?

Krishna is the greatest and nicest person known to man. So why not follow the best?

113. Will Krishna take away my sins?

Krishna won't take your sins and suffer himself, because he is God himself, and God does not suffer.

By taking shelter of Krishna and abiding by his instructions in the Bhagavad-Gita, you will stop committing sins, do everything for Krishna, instead of yourself, and change your consciousness from bodily and material to spiritual and Krishna. The result of this is that at death, Krishna will release you from all the sinful actions you have taken in millions of lives and transfer you (the soul) to the spiritual abode (Vaikuntha). There you will live in the same beautiful body eternally, full of bliss, full of knowledge, and face no problems.

"Give up all other religious beliefs and just surrender unto me [Krishna]. I will release you from all your sins. Do not worry." (Lord Krishna, Bhagavad-Gita 18.66)

114. What is the difference between Krishna and others?

The difference between Krishna and other so-called Gods or saviors is that Krishna has already appeared and saved his followers thousands of times, right here on this planet and he is so nice. If you can't make it in this life, then you will get unlimited chances (reincarnation) and you will never be sent to hell eternally. But why waste this life? Just take shelter of Krishna and make this your last miserable life.

"Those who without deviation, meditate upon me, worship me, fix their mind on me, and become attached to me, I very quickly deliver them from material existence, which is an ocean of birth, death, and miseries." (Lord Krishna, Bhagavad-Gita 12.6-7)

If you read all the scriptures on the planet, you will find that there is only one person who has actually appeared more than once, declared and proved himself as God, without any doubt. This is because,

God Is One

www.ingramcontent.com/pod-product-compliance
Lightning Source LLC
Chambersburg PA
CBHW032215040426
42449CB00005B/608